# separate
# bedrooms
# ! !

## a book about tango

by mitra martin

Dedicated to

Dad & Mom
who instilled in me joy

to

Stefan
the days, the details, and the dreams

and to
Tango Warriors of today, tomorrow,
and the next dimension.


This book exists because of so many
Tango dancers I know who are inspiring.

Here, by the way, are some of the people who in tiny
and large ways made me excited about putting forth this book:
Dave, Rebecca, Irene Nicastro, Dan R., Dad & Mom, Darius, Melika,
Chun, Anna, Richard, Rajendra, Daniel, Jaimes, Veronica, and Stefan.

With gratitude to Stephen Mitchell

# I.introductory remarks

# II.     the lexicon

# III.     the axioms of tango

12 axioms of the citizenship

21 axioms of the partnership

# IV.     challenging games

22 great challenging games that everyone can play

9 challenging games that only tango dancers can play

# INTRODUCTORY REMARKS

Hi! Okay, let's get to the bottom of this! What is this strange unit that you are holding in your hands? What you are holding is a Game, even though you cannot see any colorful wooden pieces. Did you drop them when you opened the package? No, you didn't, because they are right here, they are just existing in the fifth dimension.

You could also describe this as:

- A highly effective self-hindrance manual. Do not continue to play if you are trying to get anywhere quickly.

- A symbol of freedom! A beacon of hope! A token of peace!

- Chapter Three in the continuation of a destined love affair

- A practical guide for a few long-awaited improvements to our language, English

- An internal Olympic Games, narrated by a slightly schizophrenic ingénue commentator who has been there before

- A cataclysm for those whose workings daily emphasize the boring part of life

- The undoing of No-Hug-Zones, once and for all

- A jungle gym times a Princeton education, presented in a linguistic puppet theater

- A Tango I carried out with my computer while I was trying to figure out how to be of the best and highest service to mankind without getting hoity-toity about it

- The book version of the feature musical *"Separate Bedrooms!"* which didn't quite have enough salt, but the book did

If this Game were still shrink-wrapped, you would notice font-colored packaging that emphasizes that it is, for instance:

**An Epic Demonstrative for Happy World that will Really Last**, carried out in the deepest and most exact center of your heart and mine, against all odds, right now!

Yes! Doesn't that sound like it will just be the best? More on all that in later paragraphs and sections. And remember, Tango Warriors don't always believe the packaging.

See Also: *The Art They Playing A Game? Game*

## Personal Prelude

So I'm your average high achieving person, which means I usually like to go out and conquer really difficult stuff and get an A+. Which I've done a lot of over the course of a couple decades. And at one point it came as an annoying shock to me to realize that the MOST worthy, difficult thing to conquer out there isn't. Out there, I mean. Did you realize that too?

Well, did you take into account the existence of the fifth dimension? It may be worth trying! Some scientists are saying that there are actually *eleven* dimensions, and some of them are very tiny and folded into one another like lace. That's what my dad told me, and he reads a lot of science magazines. For the purposes of imagination let's say that the *fifth* dimension is folded up very carefully and deeply embedded inside the human.

My calculations indicate that it is located at the exact smack center of the heart, as the packaging above sort of indicates, and furthermore its radius is about equidistant to the heart and the mind. And it doesn't exist separately in separate humans; it exists centrally. I.e., if you find your way into it, you will find yourself at a REALLY GOOD PARTY.

Taking into account this quirky dimension into the overachieving things you like to do kind of causes an interesting warp-effect to happen. What I have realized is that you can't quite approach things in the same earnest way anymore, and A+ is defined differently. The game can't anymore be played through brute application of mental bandwidth; it needs a new kind of sensitivity, which to be frank I totally don't understand yet. But I think some parts of this book, when taken as a bouquet, may understand it, if I'm not mistaken. And I KNOW that the Tango understands it, and I've been hot on its tail for more than 12 years now.

## Where All This Comes From

Well it all comes from the art of the Tango, which is a concentrated distillate of *all* the truth of *all* human relationship. I don't mean Tango metaphorically; I mean it literally; as in literally, *dancing the Tango* which is what I do, mostly joyfully, for 100% of my livelihood, unless this book sells of course, in which case I may include writing a bit more.

### The 'Start Here!' Card

Actually, can we pause for a second? I find that word "Relationship," in the above paragraph, to be so long and sort of unfriendly. I really like the word "Love" a little better, don't you? That 'v' adds a kind of exotic sweetness to it and makes you think of simple pretty things; and such nice equal joinery exhibited here in the letter 'v'[1]. I guess you can use either word, just apply your vealtime thesauvus. Of course, it doesn't really matter anyway, because the pronouns and

---

[1] Or, 'r', if you're playing *Lettev Switchavoo.*

prepositions are way more important than the abstract nouns.

So anyway, the "Start Here!" card of the Game we are playing is the happy ending that maybe we all want: LOVE.

So, let's say, going along now, that you are in the process of negotiating and participating in a human duet of some kind. It doesn't matter whether you're involved in this right now, or in some future-visualisation. This may involve shared living arrangements, a rhythm of spending time and money together, contracts of an official kind, etc.

Some of you may have noticed, at this point, that this whole project of Love can, oddly, easily, straddle between being very awesome, and very toxic! Indeed, life in love can be very *extreme*. We could wonder, "Why?" but I have actually found that not to be a very helpful Wh- word. The more useful word is "When?" (For more on that, see *Tango Warriors Think Blame Is Lame.*)

*Earthlings Are Visited By Someone Helpful And Funny*

The really lucky news is that about 100 years ago a wise guide came to this four dimensional planet, Earth, with something to say about this. It crash landed in the Southern Hemisphere, and stepped out of its inter-liminal spaceship, and went to work. It came in the form of a dance, called Tango.

It is the greatest and quietest healer of our time. It is a practice for a really complicated and disconnected time! It holds deep wisdom, it is an agent of deep transformation, it is a bridge to this tiny fifth dimension where we can play the truest, realest, most worthy games that there are. It has a superb and totally opaque sense of humor.

This Tango, wisely aware of the pandemic need for its guidance, is kind enough to be highly accessible. It is the simplest and most pedestrian of dances, a folk dance created for normal folk. It can be accessed by anyone who can stand on one foot and put their arms around another person. If you can play Uno, you can play Tango. Its teaching feels strange at first and soon it feels weirdly relaxing. Once it makes friends with you, it will gently give you little five-dimensional challenge-cards that require a tidy mix of physical, emotional, and mental energy, powered by SOULAR POWER and through which you can WIN POINTS.

But while the dance itself may be the most intense experience of the alchemy, the *essence* of Tango exists with or without actually dancing. You don't need any special footwear. All you need is other people, and they are freely available in reality or in your imagination. If you subscribe, then the challenge-cards will come. This is the idea of the Tango Warrior – the person who uses every interpersonal situation available as a means to her or his own inner growth and grace.

Here it is again, boldly: the **Tango Warrior** is the person who uses every interpersonal situation available as a means to her or his own inner growth and grace!

So first terrestrial Tango Warrior that I am aware of is Rainer Maria Rilke. Talk about powerful eyes. They spook me out whenever I see a photograph! Rilke landed on the Earth around the same time as Tango, and Tango completely inhabited him even though he never owned a pair of dancing shoes. Rilke's definition of love is very Tango and very sane: two solitudes that protect and border and greet each other.

**Where all this goes to**

*Six Billion People In Love*

Some people call it Community. To me that word has too many rounded edges. I like the sharp 'Z' in the word Citizenship a little bit better. And the nice upstanding i's. It feels like there is more interesting stuff going on between the vowels, and there is that voyagey, nautical feeling. And what you realize, after some mulling and some stumbling around, is that getting your sea legs on your relation-ship may be the very perfect training ground for getting all aboard a citizen-ship that is going somewhere worth its salt.

Because, sure, we start with the two solitudes, that is the beginning and the fairy tale. And then eventually, after the happily-ever-before is fully accomplished, there may be three solitudes. And after that, eventually, you look around and there they are, all six billion solitudes, staring back at you through Google-eyes as you open your laptop and start to type in your blog. Or whatever. As you open up your hand or you start to speak. As you wake up and try to figure out what to do next, after you have taken your coffee, as you try to use a three-dimensional comb to disentangle the five-dimensional threads in your borderline alarmist mind.

Basically I want to be sane in my interactions with other people, and I have noticed (have you?) that it can be intractably challenging! Even when those other people are people I've already hugged many times! Love is needed very much in these little knots where human beings aggregate, these groups and settlements and these glass corporate offices, these places where people are wearing backpacks, these formal and informal arrangements to try to make it work together. And this Love is a close cousin of the Love I was mentioning before. And they both take practice. And Tango's numinescent technology applies to both.

Yes, let's agree, more sanity may come with practice, which is the work Tango seduces us to do: to find the strength to be sane even with the people whom

I've never hugged and who maybe even are, uh, *starting to bother me.*

## What is a Tango Warrior, Again?

So basically, a Tango Warrior is a new kind of life partner and simultaneously a new kind of citizen. The kind of partner and citizen that everyone intends, someday, to be or wants, someday, to find. These pages hold a character sketch intended to dissolve that 'someday' into someday *soon* and/or Right Now. For myself as well as for anyone else who picks it up. They amply reflect the very very difficult time I am having as I personally struggle with my little challenge-cards (of course with intention to immediately WIN); as I try very hard to become that partner and become that citizen, and sometimes slack off.

I wish this concoction of lingustic matter to become some kind of a touchstone for undercover Tango Warriors all over the place to come out and find and connect to each other and help each other fight this very good (and did I mention, very sexy?) fight. Oh. I think I did not mention that yet! It's very, very sexy, too.

## Remember, This Is A Game. A Very, Very, Difficult Game.

Lest we get too hunkered-down and serious, I'd like to propose that we not do that. Seriousness is a stance and it is somewhat cramping sometimes.

Sometimes we say 'I Need To Get Serious' but what would really help is actually just focusing on one single thing until it is better. And you can focus on it while staying a little amused, which would feel nicer probably.

'Healing' sounds fancy and expensive and vague, it sounds like a big scary technique, it will take lots of time. So do things like this: 'meditation', 'practice', 'self-improvement'. Etc. Abstract nouns, again. We don't know where they begin and where they end! *Games*, however, have a specific beginning and a specific ending. *Games* are celebrations of specificity, obviously, because there are *rules! Games* are a mix of being serious and unserious in the right proportions. *Games* are inherently educational, self-improving, and quieting over the long run.

For Tango Warriors, games are a lifestyle. Whatever it is, we play or invent a game that goes with it. Some games are games we play with ourselves. Some we play with our partner. Some we are playing all the time with everyone. The dance called the Tango is one big game that involves everyone, a fact which is true even if you didn't notice already. Hilariously, it is in disguise as something really super important, way more important than a game, something that has to do with *the future of the species via sexual reproduction, and also enlightenment.* Being in disguise is actually a delightful resource, since that makes it more theatrical, funny, and harder to play. Hard games are more alchemical. Hard games are more worth learning. *Perche più dificile é più bello!*

That's what they told me, when I was dancing Tango in Milan.

## Tango as a Dance

I am going to explain Tango *dancing* here via a few bulleted lists.

*Bulleted List #1*

Here's how Tango works.
1. There is something you want very dearly:
    a. A person you want to be close to
    b. A way-of-being (e.g., beauty, love, something smoothly carved) that you want to embody

2. Via the conduit of other people, you get hints and snatches of an experience that makes you feel closer to this dearness and also totally high;

3. Now suddenly you feel very very far away from it, totally insurmountably far, like you are Kafka and everything has turned strange *and* you're getting your period[2];

4. Repeat 2 & 3, for a long time;

5. You learn, by trial and error and intense work

---

[2] This metaphor applies to you *especially* if you are a boy reading this, and *no*, this book is not written just for girls

and helpful inputs, the particular skills that enable you to *relatively reliably* create that really nice experience for yourself, which is what makes it palpable for the other ones around you;

6. You realize that you are now a magician and it is tempting to start to abuse this power, but you don't anymore because after doing so a few times you realize that it sucks;

7. And now there is something you want very dearly.

That's basically it. It's just like normal life frankly, but a bit more intensified. It's exactly what happens on Facebook and in your workplace, but more artistic, psychedelic, and vavoom. It's vavoom because, instead of just IM-ing with someone who's beautiful and inaccessible, you are dancing with zhem[3], which means you are pressing your heart next to zheir heart, which means there is a transfusion of love going on and that you are achieving a five-dimensional splendor together!

---

[3] See also *The Lexicon* for definitions of crucial words you may not know yet.

*Bulleted List #2*

Here are the usual traps that Tango sets out and this is how it all starts, WATCH OUT!

1. A woman whose accent is so innocent, her buttons are so small, and you want to hold her.

2. A man who could be out smashing things or yawning but isn't; instead his movement and way of holding things makes you think that trees can dance and maybe that's what he is.

3. Two people, in fabrics that flow and prowl, making the full nuance of their love, round with restraint, visible for YOU!

*Bulleted List #3*

Again, Tango dancing is not that different from regular going out, it's just more schmoflisticlated[4]. Technically, a Tango party is magic and here are the rules of the theater:

- If you are broiling and want to steep something in your LOVE, you can, but first you need to get that

---

[4] See the section entitled *Challenging Games I: For The Generalist*, which encloses a complete decoder ring for some of the ways I like to use language that aren't likewise apparent (although you can probably figure this one out). This is an example of the lucky game called *Smig Blatin, or the 'I Glove You' Game.*

thing's permission. Steeping is done in many ways but it is done best via nearness.

- How to bring one thing or person near to another thing or person is an exercise of infinite artistry. Sort of like tea ceremonies. You know the leaves are going to be brought into the broiling water, eventually, but HOW??

- The answer to the question HOW??, in all capital letters, is the beginning of an adventure which, crucially, involves Your Eyes and the skillful use themof.

- All of this, the tea, the broiling water, the mystery of Your Eyes, this is what makes the weekend fun and makes it worthwhile for a human to be nocturnal, which otherwise is a very unnatural mode. Daytimes are made for washing and ironing our imaginary red capes, drinking coffee, and torturing ourselves with the development of New Skills, whereby we make life more fun at night.

- If it so happens that, through successful application of my infinite artistry and New Skills, I put my arms around you, and you put your arms around me, an equation of deep equivalence is activated.

- If you think in terms of 'how can I make this whole tea party nicer for everyone else,' then you are most likely to be on the right track.

- Something will be unplannable and will not quite fit into the matrix of desire, and it is exactly this thing that may bring the poetry into the night.

So that's Tango. Basically it's the answer to the question: if I want to put my arms around you, somebody beautiful, and walk around a room that is full of other people doing the same, how do I do that? And, but, it's oh so much more; see above.

PS. If you want to see living Tango dancing, you should go to a *milonga*. There is probably one tonight, a few minutes away from where you live, and The Google can help you find it.

## Where We Go From Here

Now, not everyone has the time and bandwidth to learn how to dance Tango, which is cool, because maybe you are doing other really useful things on this planet.

Whatever those useful things are, though, if they are putting you in touch with other people, which they do, you might be more fun and effective if you do them in the spirit of a Tango Warrior.

What you have in the next section, which is the biggest and most central part of the book called *Separate Bedrooms ! !,* is a mosaic of things that Tango told me over the past 12 years, which I try to apply to the parallel voyages of relation-ship and citizen-ship.

It is basically a Code of Conduct and Self-Management that comes from the wise and hilarious dance of the Tango, which can, in a strong case-scenario, help you steer your ships, whichever waters they are in. Have fun!

# LEXICON

When Tango arrived here on earth, it brought with it a lexicon of reenchantment that is in use among Tango Warriors. These words may be helpful to you as you learn the ways of the Tango Warrior.

All the words here were recorded by the Center for Proactive Grammatical Technology, as sort of US-based lunfardo crusade, where they we are working closely with beings from higher dimensions, such as Tango, to revitalize English grammar.

My understanding is that the CPGT's aim is to develop the grammatical technology that human beings need in order to explore the spacetime continuum in a more empowered way. Good luck!

*The Prepositions:*

*Ky* – kAI, The relation of being geographically or spatially separate from someone and simultaneously emotionally close to them (naturally and mutually so) as if caressing or inhabiting the same music.

*Pryn* – prEn, The relation of being physically propinquitous to someone while also being simultaneously mutually emotionally estranged from one another, *as if* on separate sun-systems or living out mutually unintelligible fables.

*Anander* – enAnder, The relation of two or more

individuals making mitigated partial-hearted efforts to achieve synchrony with one another but without quite putting enough energy into achieving thus due to other considerations and motives, creating an interesting kind of stutter-effect.

*Atroth* – etrOth. Connected to another human person as kin through immediate taut relational lines drawn in higher dimensions, manifested through the experience of immediate recognition of them as if from a dream world.

*Athwaite* – ethwAIT, Connected as if by pact to another human person whose presence, spatial or imagined, most often unwittingly and without their participation, creates an extreme paralyzing and/or crushing intensity of emotion/inner turbulence in the subject, also known as "freaking out[5]" around someone

*Atwain* – eTWAYN, Connected to another human person via irrevocable decision.

*The Pronouns:*

*VELK* – VELK, The adorably grandiose self: the one who lives in LA and does amazing things, including traveling to New York from time to time and saying words like 'property consciousness.' VELK mostly uses abstract nouns and extreme adjectives, in a loud hallway voice. VELK is loveably clueless, and through

---

[5] While looking cool

the letters of its pronoun achieves both VELK-aggrandization and VELK-mockery. VELK takes a plural conjugation, as in "VELK Want Sushi!" and "VELK Need to Consult with iPhone." Yes, in fact VELK can use capital letter whenever VELK want to. Articles and other little words are only semi-necessary around VELK.

*VUSK* – VUSK, The affably grandiose couple. VUSK is formed by a cordial couple of VELKEN who are joined by habit and usually seen together. VUSK is blindingly light-emitting! VUSK makes you wonder so many things about it! VUSK wears interesting clothing together, and of course VUSK dances a mean Tango! Naturally, because VUSK is moving with so much motive energy, VUSK takes a plural verb and beyond this often utilizes Auxiliary Verb Redundancy, and in many cases, optional Main Verb Redundancy! "VUSK Are Are Going to Go Have Sex!" Or, if VUSK is feeling especially holiday, "VUSK Are Are Going Going to Go Have Sex!! Sex!!" Indeed, reduplication of any kind is possible, around VUSK. One other feature of VUSK is that you usually will not know which one to call.

*Wowr* – wow-er, possessive pronoun, belonging to VELK or VUSK. It should sound kind of like you are roaring in an affectionate way![6]

*neveryone* – NEV-ri-wun, Everyone except VUSK. The

---

[6] That's specifically how they pronounce it at the place where this term, along with VUSK, was first fabricated: The JesuChrista Tango Factory. Which is perfect, since VUSK Looks Looks Upon Wowr Inventions & Are Are Glad !

dedicated, educated, sometimes slightly wounded loneliness of VUSK. neveryone gossips so much! neveryone throws such lame parties! neveryone eats such non-nutritive foods usually! neveryone's there already! "who, if VUSK cried, cried out, would hear VUSK among the angel's hierarchies?" The answer is, of course, that *neveryone would.* Sometimes it is hard being VUSK, because of how hard it is for neveryone to understand you, and for neveryone to reach you on the telephone, due to their uncertainty about which number to dial.

*Zhem* – zhEM, personal pronoun which refers to the person with whom one is decisively romantically connected, either *atroth* or *atwain.* This is a compact, sexy, and also gender neutral way to refer to "your partner;" "your boyfriend/girlfriend;" "him/her with whom I am in a relationship;" or, worse, "they/them". This pronoun is used by self-help authors abound. For instance: "If your partner is angry with you, it's a good idea to hug zhem immediately."

# THE AXIOMS OF TANGO

## 12 AXIOMS
## OF THE CITIZENSHIP

### Tango Warriors Are Festive

Alone, in pairs, or in groups, Tango Warriors exhibit such qualities as luminosity, boisterousness, and headdresses. You will often find them dressing up as someone else, or in some cryptic way in order to attract attention and/or create a game and/or for no reason. This brings a quality of awesomeness to the moments of each day.

As often as not, Tango Warriors inhabit places that can be dim or even a tiny bit déclassé, like old restaurants or walkup apartments, where a brightening festivity is especially called for.

Festivity permeates their communications. Tango Warriors enjoy erring on the side of formality, because it is more unusual. They may take their leave of you, with exquisite detail, in the laundry room; confirming the coordinates of your next rendezvous (perhaps, notating it down on their moleskin-bound planner); and reconvene wearing an asymmetrical waistcoat, on the south side of the kitchen.

Tango Warriors also are in the habit of giving very very exciting gifts to each other, like mittens or cupcakes or mismatched socks, persistently, ideally at a totally unexpected occasion, such as Grammatical Liberation Day (May 2nd).

In the old days, their favorite interjection was: "La!," which they are currently trying to revive. If in doubt, chant the Tango Warrior sing-a-long song: "If it's fun, it's fun. If it's not, it's not." Real people whose haven't been hypno-anaesthetized by PowerPoint misuse can usually tell the difference!

## Tango Warriors Don't Cut You Off

Tango Warriors are fun to be around because they are socially conscious. Socially conscious in a very concrete way. Like, they might not be sending laptop computers to Africa on a daily basis, but they will be scrupulous about how what they are doing affects the people around them.

For instance, Tango Warriors often find themselves in a lot of assertive traffic, and here they always exhibit the most exquisite manners. Unequivocally they protect the individual seated beside them, and they help the other drivers protect their cargo.

This is because Tango Warriors are addicted to the beauty of a particular five-dimensional shape which is called a *ronda*. A *ronda* is the shape made by many couples living and dancing harmoniously together. It is sort of like a tunnel and sort of like a tesseract and highly alchemical.

See Also: *Tango Warriors Are the Best Hosts*

## Tango Warriors Curb Their Emissions

Whatever the science says or doesn't say, Tango Warriors know first hand that emissions are just gross. Too many emissions means no more dancing for you. People with many emissions are simply known to be rather foul and, for the time being, are gently dis- included via eye contact withholdment. This means that there are far fewer opportunities for, well, pretty much anything creative. No matter how sexy you are, irresponsible emissions makes you rather grotesque. This is also true of countries.

Tango Warriors also know that you can easily avoid disgusting emissions by making intelligent choices about what, when, and how much you choose to consume. It is much harder to clamp down on persistent, cheeky emissions when you are trying to process things that were never meant to be digested by natural systems.

## Tango Warriors are Picky Media Eaters

When Tango Warriors go out to buy their media groceries, they have certain recipes in mind already. These recipes have been passed down by elders and they are really delicious. Most of the items sold at regular big-box media supermarkets are not suitable, and often these mass-market items create a lot of gross emissions too.

So instead, Tango Warriors they do their shopping mostly at small independent farmers' media markets that offer a nice affordable selection of whole grain films, organic anime roughage, and free-range facts, as well as locally-grown paradox. Using these ingredients, they are able to concoct a stable environment for the establishment of their AXIS.

See Also: *Tango Warriors Have Separate Bedrooms For Some Good Information about Your AXIS*

## Tango Warriors Actually Get Enough Sleep
### In Their Own Bedroom, Sometimes

*"Sleep is the best meditation.*
*It should be approached with reckless abandon"*

~His Holiness, the Dalai Lama

This is quite straightforward. The average Tango Warrior needs roughly eight hours of sleep in order to meet the many intrepid inner and outer exigencies they choose to carry out. Therefore, when they go to bed, Tango Warriors check the current time and set their alarm clock for eight hours later. If these eight hours occur during daylight hours, they use darkening cloth on their windows. Sometimes it happens that Tango Warriors become occupied in acts of warriordom that require wakefulness during this interval of time, whereupon they stay in bed a little longer.

See Also: *The Game of Elastic Time*

## Tango Warriors are The Best Hosts

One is a host whether their guest is in their arms or in their spare bedroom. Tango Warriors practice impeccable detail of welcome either way. Here are the factors that the best hosts attend to: warmth (blankets; hugs); freedom (in the form of spare keys and local intelligence about where the coffeeshop is); clear boundaries; access to appropriate and timely nourishment; spells of laughter. Creating a climate that provides these things requires an earnest commitment to them, *la!* Hosts and guest are recommended to play *The Game of Randomly Interchangeable Pronouns*, at all times. We also think they should go for a long walk together, at some point if that's possible. And a large pineapple is always in order.

The presence of a guest may sometimes cause a host to feel low levels of irritation, judgement, and inconvenience, especially if they show up late and we can't find the pump for the air mattress. Or, if, say, they misplaced their AXIS and totally can't find it. These types of situations are fantastic, because they are an opportunity to pratice Tango Warriordom, which, did we mention, is defined as "using every interpersonal situation available as a means to achieve your own inner growth and grace."

When a guest is (hopefully inadvertently and only slightly) egregious, Tango Warrior Hosts blithely verbalize their retaliatory measures over breakfast, which may entail for instance, levying a Shampoo Tax (utilizing guests' high-end botanical hair products.) Dimensionally insouciant guests are of course the most challenging, but Tango needs them too, so we host them with good grace, if and when we are up to it.

Being a guest is naturally an art form in itself, as the host will understand via the practice of playing *The Game* and also via traveling the world.

## Tango Warriors And Drugs

Bribery and substances. By the way, Tango is, I hate to tell you, a powerful, powerful drug lord who every day labors to elicit chemical dependency within a cult of followers, including you, including me, for geopolitical motives.

It's called Oxytocin. Tango Warriors are addicted to the stuff. It's their favorite chemical to support optimal brain alchemistry. They prefer it to any vintage, any preparation or any powder, any molecule that can be administered in any way. And, it is conveniently manufactured for free right inside of their organic bodies under the right circumstances.

Which are: hugging.

Total addictiveness is only one dimension of this drug; it also has several additional idiosyncracies that Tango Warriors love, all relating to oxytocin's aggressive antitoxicity. For instance, no matter how high one's Blood Oxytocin Level, one can still safely drive the people they love from here to there; it gives an amazing, exotic high of total completeness without any malaise or de-nutritive side-effects at all, neither now nor later; and, it is free, even during the recession.

For these reasons, under adverse or self-sabotaging circumstances, Tango Warriors are known to immediately find someone who can administer the right environment for an Oxytocin shot (one hug equaling no less than 20 seconds in duration) which is an excellent tool for feeling good immediately afterwards. It also works like a blanket or fleece, it makes you feel warmer.

Now many times in this click-centric and cool culture, you may find yourself in an Oxytocin-Impoverished Environment. To the extent that twenty-second hugs are unavailable inside of the places you exist, our institutions are failing us. I once heard of a girl who walked into a corporate office and not only she did not get any HUG *at all* for almost six years, there were days that she did not even get practically any eye contact either, for most of the time! Now granted, she was slightly on the shy side and could have wrought her own hugs if she had had the right training. But in any case, the Tango would consider this an abusive environment and is actively working with leading thinkers to do something about it, so that everyone has immediate facility at their disposal to achieve correct brain alchemistry to partipate in *la ronda*.

## Tango Warriors Are Flirts!

But do you know what flirting *is*? Flirting is a beautifully simple *game* with real stakes. Here is how you lose the game: by forgetting that that's all it is. Here is how you win: you are given a swift gift, a moment of unexpected intimacy, such as going on a walk with your friend whom you like and arriving in a surprisingly green garden. It gets dark, he looks at your face, a hair longer than he did five minutes ago when he was your friend. He tells you about how his rage works, you find an interesting bug.

Flirting is an extremely useful practice for all involved. In the hands of the Tango its purpose is to teach us the skills we need to assure our own emotional safeness at all times. Its role is to lightly destabilize us so that we can restabilze ourselves with our own *technique*. Its role is to seduce us momentarily into passivity so that we can immediately reorganize ourselves to remember who actually creates the magic around here.

See Also: *Tango Warriors Know Where The Magic Comes From*

## Tango Warriors Are Kissing Minimalists

Tango Warriors feel that there is a surplus of kissing going on. People who are in organized human ensembles are, by and large, overkissed and overkissing. And there is nowhere to store all the extra kisses, which by now constitute a veritable plethora.

For this reason, Tango Warriors are kissing minimalists. They have noticed that *not* kissing can often be even more evocative than kissing; that kissing less can be more *interesting* than kissing more. For this reason, Tango Warriors have a wooden game-board called *la pista* where kissing is, by general agreement and by severe injuction of the wise Tango itself, totally not allowed.

Once you wax on and off this proposition, as Tango directs, you will learn the main point of this challenge-card has less to do with kissing and more to do with something the French call *jouissance*, if we are understanding this term correctly. Ancillarily and in related news, Tango Warriors notice what quickly happens when you take the letters n, s, u, a, t, and i, out of the word 'consummation,' and Tango Warriors tend to prefer more unusual sensations than that.

We are being very indirect here, and that is because Tango is very indirect in this area. Tango allows that you don't need to live your whole life on the game-board. Just like human chess pieces, of course there are times when we step off the game board, remove our festive crowns, take a shower and kiss and kiss.

But Tango simultaneously reminds us that the game-board is where a good helping of most *interesting* intensity is going to happen. Where we will have exquisite and unforgettable consummations, guided expertly by the third intelligence, that do not involve any bodily fluids at all except a little bit of perspiration. Between people who don't have any plans to formalize any human duet with each other after they step off of *la pista*. Between people who are simply atroth one another. Eventually, we Warriors get used to love that tatters the breath without ever, ever, touching the lips, and we allow ourselves to be surprised by the many and unexpected forms in which it comes. Which, may I say, adds a very sharp dimension of salted beauty to our Citizen Ship.

See Also: *Tango Warriors Listen for the Third Intelligence; The Tango Warriors' Flag*

## Tango Warriors Are Circles Within Circles

What is politics? Politics is anything that fosters the religion called Cynicism. In this religion, people actually believe that the way the world is working is somehow really incorrect.

Tango Warriors don't like anything that's more organized than necessary for the Game to work—organized religion being maybe one of those things—and Cynicism itself is indeed quite tightly organized within the human mental interpretational system. In order to avoid the promulgation of Cynicism, therefore, they have developed an alternative to politics which *superficially* looks a bit political but has very different effects, namely, innocence.

It's called *Circles Within Circles.* The working assumption is called *"if it's not working, I can do better."* The orthodox cynic will say "It's not working, the system and the chessmen who make it up, they are at fault." Quickly or slowly, this becomes boring. But the innocent Warrior will say this: "it's not working; I can do better." Through this they acquire access into more and more subtle realms of the five-dimensional galaxy of the interior. Including especially, the nebulas. The nebulas are the coolest.

In normal geometric terms, the fifth dimension is made up of concentric circles, and all of them have the same radius which is of course the key measure, the distance between your heart and your mind. We find the radius by measuring the full diameter, using a ruler that marks out both metric musicality and imperial ruthlessness, then dividing it in two. Then we can find the circumference by multiplying by pi. The one with the smallest circumference is the one that Death wants to show us in this lifetime, and we will have to work very hard to get there in time. Get there in time. You can't if you are a fundamentalist cynic.

What I am saying is that they don't owe it to you, in fact they will make you fight for it, and that is as it should be. Fight for membership, and you find the nebulas that dazzle you with the way their dust glitters and makes shapes.

Some historians believe that the very word *Tango* means, "closed space", "circle", "any private space to which one must ask permission to enter". We can assume that we want to be inside, and more inside, and more and more inside. The real question is, who are we asking permission from? Kafka? Watch out; you may be playing games your whole life. But that wouldn't be so bad, either. Here are the concentric game boards:

- The circle of everyone who is consistently *ky* you

- The circle of Tango Warriors

- The circle of the ones who are dancing, in this room, right now

- The circle that is created with my arms and your arms, right now, where she and he – separately and together – are immersed – always – in the embodiment of the round ocean of Mozart to the Di Sarli-th power. What does that mean? If you want to know, keep dancing until you find out.

See Also: *Tango Warriors Know It Will End*

## Tango Warriors And Moon-Time

Friends: I am not sure where to put this section, but it definitely concerns the whole ship, so here it is. It may make some people wince if they are feeling preferential to festive-times as opposed to words such as "awfulness" and "doom" which are comprised here below. Sometimes life *is* messy though, and I think our ship will steer better if we know about it together.

Okay, so, Moon-Time is defined, by me, as approximately the *main day of the month* when a woman's intrauterine lining, along with all her illusions of any kind, are being actively shedded. Basically a big chunk of her body is leaving her body, and that is how it feels. It is bittersweet and really messy. Bitter because it is proof that that particular conglomeration of intrauterine lining is definitely no longer going to sustain any new living cute person who would have someday populated the Citizen Ship and laughed. Sweet because we're making some space and that always feels good. Often it is accompanied by a non-imaginary sense of strongly impending awfulness that nobody can understand if they aren't female, but they should try to anyway. I have heard that even the most frantically high-achieving female people, like me sometimes, are during this time able to sit and do nothing but look at the way the leaves are moving. And that is what I am doing now.

Two or three important things of note:

- The job of the male people during Moon-Time is to be exactly like Stefan. He can tell you the exact right mix, but it definitely involves: strong arms that give everlasting hugs to people who are spiky and angry and directly experiencing doom, until the doom kind of dissolves, until tomorrow.

- The job of our social institutions during this time, including workplaces that have the word Inc. or LLC or .gov in their name, is to ask our women to please STOP answering emails and to instead look at the leaves and how they are moving and garner whatever wisdom is possible from that experience, and to bring this wisdom back with them, in the form of an emanation or mood, that may somehow guide the social institution and future quarterly statements. There needs to be a special Out-Of-Office Automated Assistant to delicately explain the importance of this.

- The job of women during Moon-Time is to notice how easy it is to feel guilty about all this, and to NOT, and to instead just get a hot water bottle and find a window to curl next to.

# The Tango Warriors' Flag

Okay, wrapping up now! You have participated a lot in a festive, salty, round and slightly confusing Tango on a teetering Citizen Ship for the past twenty pages or so. Did it suck? Was it sublime? Or was it (most likely) something in between? Did you judge zhem a little tiny bit? Did you feel like you could barely keep up, were you distracted? Did you emote internally, did you endeavor to mysticalize things, did you maybe get some masturbatory pleasure out of being better than zhem? We are trying, we are human beings, it is awkward to connect, there are a thousand traps we must learn about.

Yes, *my* great flirtations, my tandas and my liaisons, they are all me being a badass version of my favorite fairy-tale character and maybe they'll make a movie of it. Yes, *my* Tango has got *my* tragedy built into its DNA, the tragedy of life-missed-out-on, and we all have it. Yes, there are all these stories and yes they will fill your mind until they don't anymore, until The Connection is intact and you can decant your technique from the cloudy me-water it's sitting in.

In the meanwhile, at the end of the dance, and every dance ends, there is only one thing left: gratitude.

There are three kinds of Thank You, but only one that is useful to the Tango Warrior.

1. Tango Dancers and other people sometimes utilize "thank you" as a formula which

means "I am done with you now."

2.  There is a sentimental "Thank You" which is
    a resonance chamber for all the beautiful
    details zhey gave to one another: that
    smallest and most secret sigh, which he
    gave you after you bloomed and poured
    together in the imperfect Pugliese weather;
    the rocks you sat on then; the unforgettable
    shape of his scapula and the way it felt to
    accidentally hold his arm under the tee shirt
    sleeve. Normally this kind of Thank You is
    rather asymmetrical, because Tango Warriors
    seldom have identical or reciprocal
    emotional experiences despite dancing
    magnificently together. There is a whole
    section on this, by the way, called: *Tango
    Warriors Love Asymmetry.*

3.  The Tango Warrior Thank You. With this
    one, we are "thanking you" for all the gentle
    things that you did that made my world
    difficult for me. In this way we affirm the
    Warrior's Process in one another. This Thank
    You is the Tango Warrior's flag, with bold
    authentic colors, that reminds us that we
    are all working on the same thing. It
    operates as a salute, a reciprocal infusion of
    power. Here are some examples:

    o  Thank you for the way your presence
       ripened me by letting me want you and
       not letting me have you.

- It was very hard dancing with you, thank you for the opportunity to become stronger through dealing with [the charming way in which you blame/amplify/emote/sabotage/gaze at me; your adolescent AXIS; your comic emissions, etc.]

Dancing Tango, which we are doing together right now, holds the potential for an intensity that closely parallels the fullest experience of being alive. For the opportunity to have a shot at this, *I Really Thank You!* I don't want anything more. You allowed me to dance. Heart.

This page is left sort of blank. Think it over!

# 21 AXIOMS
# OF THE PARTNERSHIP

(THIS IS THE HARD PART. *LA!*)

## Tango Warriors Know
## Where the Magic Comes From

You are waiting for something to happen.

Usually, you are waiting to fall in love. You are waiting to be flooded with 'that feeling.'

You are waiting and waiting, and waiting.

The reason you are waiting like this for love, and trying always to decide if it has come or if it has not, is because of ill-constructed metaphors. Our metaphors of Love are mostly metaphors of passivity, as the brilliant mind of George Lakoff pointed out back in the '60s. We think Love is some madness that bites us, some hole we fall into, some long confusing journey, some object which we cannot find. Are these metaphors constructive? No, Tango Warriors do not think these metaphors are constructive.

Because Tango Warriors are not waiting. They are not pretending that Love's *out there somewhere*, half tease and half terrorist, waiting around to decide I am worthy. Tango has taught them that that 'that feeling' is something that YOU CAN CREATE for yourself and for others too. Their metaphor is this: Love is a collaborative work of art. And in a collaborative work of art, the magic comes from where? Technique. Your own technique. What you do, every day.

Tango teaches us that technique is damn sexy. And technique is within your control. And you work on it continuously. And you work on it at every stage of your duet.

Ah it is so easy to sigh and say, "I'm just not feeling it anymore with you. The love that bit and swallowed me up, the love that threw me down and addled my mind and put me in a thickety hormone maze, well I don't know where it is anymore, it seems to have gone away completely and I just don't feel that feeling, that magic, that stuff that everyone tells me I should feel if I want to call it love."

Tango Warriors are skeptical. If they don't feel it, they take it upon themselves. Why? Because it's more difficult to do this. And in the world of Tango Warriors, the more difficult thing is the cooler thing. It would be *easy*, you see, to say that "The Love Has Gone And I Can't Do Anything About It." It would be so *easy* to say "She is boring me, she is supposed to be a magic entertainment channel and she just didn't invest enough in programming, where's the remote." What is *difficult* is to say: "I can do better."

She will not always be balanced. He will not always

make you feel safe. You guys will not feel 'that feeling' all the time. How rich! How kind of Tango to go out of its way, to come to our planet, to show us that we have the power to create 'that feeling' ourselves through practice.

## Tango Warriors Have Powerful Eyes

 This is a photograph of the German poet Rainer Maria Rilke, one of the world's first, finest, and most articulate Tango Warriors. Gaze, for a moment, into his eyes. He is asking you to dance.

Tango Warriors use words in a very specific way. They take care not to use words when the message can be communicated more clearly via the eyes.

See Also: *Tango Warriors Are Decisive*
*Tango Warriors Don't Emote*
*Tango Warriors are a Tiny Bit Suspicious of Words*

## Tango Warriors Cultivate GOOD Tension.
## (Never Weird Tension.)

Hi Jill,

I loved our dancing. I am sorry I had to leave without saying 'bye! I hadn't realized that the carpool crew was leaving quite so promptly. I hope we have a chance to connect again sometime soon, like maybe at the St. Louis festivities.

Robert

*The above is a simple example of a Tango Warrior utilizing the intrinsic specificity of words to defuse and dismantle a potentially weird tension.*

* *

*The above is a simple example of a Tango Warrior NOT utilizing the intrinsic specificity of words in order to cultivate GOOD tension.*

Get it? Only you, Tango Warrior, know when a few words are needed in order to avoid weird tension and find better economy of motion.

Likewise, only you know when you can create GOOD, pleasant, mysterious tension by skipping the application of words altogether. Choose carefully, but remember it doesn't really matter much either way, because the duet already has its own unreal five-dimensional Möbius shape, which, did I mention, includes all the awkward things you have ever said or done to someone you liked or who liked you.

See also: *Tango Warriors are a Tiny Bit Suspicious of Words*
and
*Tango Warriors Don't Emote*

### Tango Warriors Know it will End

"*Makinu mamfumu ka mazingilana ko*"
– Ki-Kongo saying
"No matter how noble, no dance is forever."

Duets encompass death.

Tango knows this and teaches it to us all the time, every day, all the time.

Very common it is for us to start dancing with someone and actually fantasize that it will last forever, either in duration, or via being of such a totally epic quality that it will be celebrated eternally in oral tradition, or via a small package called 'children.'

What's true, in fact, is that each relationship between two humans has a definitive and distinct shape *with edges*. From the point of view of the dimensionally non-insouciant[7], I hear, it looks sort of like a rhizome; sort of like a donut; and built into in its DNA is the index of an atlas of celestial navigation written by Luigi Serafini. This thing is non-edible and does not biodegrade. It is there regardless of what happens in the four-dimensional frame, and when we decisively enage into a duet, our job is to only feel out and fill in the unreal contours of this pre-existing form. Which isn't infinite.

Since we have the chance, it's nice to inhabit the donut-rhizome thing as convincingly as possible, which is actually easier once you know it's going to stop. And if everyone is doing that, then when somebody hits an edge there is reason for festivity.

Tango calls the festivity of death *La Cumparsa*. Or, perhaps more humbly, *La Cumparsita*. *La Cumparsita* is a collective experience which Tango discovered in the sane and joyful kingdoms of Mbaza Kongo and Lwangu and gently introduced to its first lost and scared Warriors in Patagonia.

---

[7] R. Buckminster Fuller, for instance

It holds an intrinsic ecstasy and an intrinsic disenchantment. It contains awe. It is ideally performed at around 5am with the fluorescent lights on and lots of half-empty cups everywhere. *La Cumparsita* is the most difficult thing for Tango Warriors who do not dance to access but its fragrance can be noted via the contemplation of orange trees. Also, Di Sarli knows, so you could ask him.

By the way, see also:
*Tango Warriors Listen for The Third Intelligence*

## Tango Warriors are
## Infinitely Curious about Prepositions

"Do you consider love the strongest emotion?"

"Do you know a stronger?"

"Yes: *interest.*"

-Thomas Mann, *Doctor Faustus*[8]

Prepositions are tiny little words that help us describe the different nuances of *Relationship* between items, or people. Near, aft, underneath, amidst, throughout, between. Tango Warriors consider these the most interesting words in any language.

---

[8] The one translated by H. T. Lowe-Porter, and published by Viking International, which I read for my mindaltering Comparative Lliterature class with Stanley Corngold, in which among other unforgettable things is a scene in which three children examine a leaf butterfly.

Tango Warriors who also happen to dance, for instance, will get together and endlessly investigate a question like 'How *near* should I be to her when we do that?' 'Should my hips turn *toward* him here, or *away*?' 'How far *beyond* my standing leg should my ribcage go, in order to keep connected?' Questions like this are not completely without moments of champagne spaciousness which are almost better than kissing.

Oftentimes, the dancers apply to elders for advice. Prepositional understanding is something that is almost necessarily deeper with age, and most of our elders have got good quality theories on things like when you should be right *beside* him vs. when you should go *away* from him, and how much space should generally be *between* you both if you want to be able to do interesting things together.

Infinite curiosity is a resource, because it allows us to play roles that we wouldn't maybe otherwise play. For instance, most Tango Warriors find the abstract terms 'masculine' and 'feminine' to be questionable little buckets. In order to satisfy their curiosity, they are always drawn to swap roles for the time being. This brings a level of novelty, amusement, compassion, and ultimately yields better understanding of one another.

For instance, in your household, it may be that one of you does the driving, and the other of you entertains the driver with story and song, so that he doesn't fall asleep. In the cars of Tango Warriors, it is considered fun to enact a positional switch for the day and see how that feels. New positions means new prepositions; now I'll be fore and you'll be aft. Through applying this consistently in many different contexts[9], they eventually (1) like each other better and (2) find cooler ways to do the same old things and (3) create a home for the couples' AXIS in the fifth dimension. You can tell you have reached this state, when there is a harmonious blend of yinitiative and preceptivity in each Warrior individually, as well as in the duet as a unit.

## Tango Warriors are Decisive

In the world of Tango Warriors, love happens via irrevocable decision. There are two decisions of import:

1. The decision to create a duet form at all. This decision is communicated directly to the spirits out there usually without reference to any particular person.
2. The decision to create a duet with *zhem* specifically. This decision is communicate directly to *zhem* in person & with eye contact.
   a. This decision sparks the possibility of a decision by zhem, which may lead to a dance.

---

[9] E.g., Switching sides of the bed that you sleep on; switching who does the bills and who does the laundry; switching bedrooms; etc.

Every dance is invited and then accepted, or refused. Tango Warriors show respect for each invitation by providing a Yes that means Yes, or No that means No.

Each Tango Warrior makes each of these decisions (1 and 2, OR 1 and 2a) separately, and with a sense of gravitas. Once decisions #2 and #2a are made, if they happen to interlock, both Tango Warriors stand by them with a sense of the honorable national security.

While Tango Warriors are dancing together, literally or metaphorically, they experience a thing called 'exclusive commitment.' There is no room for decision deployment re-evaluation, wandering or waffling. And even if they find one another emotionally problematic at some point, which is can be predicted to happen without fail, they know that their decision to duet together is bigger than whatever they are feeling, thinking, or tempted by. This is what it means for two people to be atwain each other.

See Also: *Tango Warriors Know Where The Magic Comes From*

## Tango Warriors Have Separate Bedrooms

Tango Warriors are happy people because they know that being *part of a duet* and being *independent of the duet* are mutually inclusive. And simultaneous.

Duets, including marriage, have simultaneous

coexisting schemes of logic. Our destiny as individual warriors is to express ourselves authentically and totally within the parameters of our species and culture. And our destiny as Tango Warriors is to express ourselves authentically and totally within the parameters of species, culture, and couple.

To express ourselves authentically we must know at all times that we are born alone, we will die alone, we will look at orange trees alone. These principles are true, *even if somebody offers to wrap zheir arms around us until death do do us part.*

What this means technically is that Tango Warriors can stand up without being held up. We have a relationship with the Earth and gravity which you could call Balance. It can be fun to test the limits of this, for instance by standing on one foot and/or wearing four inch heels and/or noticing that *someone* picked up the totally wrong brand of blasphemic vinegar at the store. What we notice by testing it is that it seems to work best when the different parts of our skeleton, muscular, and mental systems have a harmonious relationship with each other. Which you could call Alignment. Balance and Alignment are extremely dynamic things! Together, they comprise what Tango would call THE AXIS.

THE AXIS needs a home, and its home is your bedroom, and each bedroom has room for a single AXIS. The bedroom is its lair and locus of strength. It emerges from the bedroom, strong, sexy, and ready to dance. Sometimes, it is feeling great and invites the friendly strong and sexy AXIS that is atwain it, into its bedroom.[10]

Some people ask if the couple has its own AXIS, and thus needs its own bedroom. The answer is, definitely! Yes! But as the couples' AXIS exists in five dimensions, instead of four, its bedroom need not take up space in your three- to four-dimensional house.

We think it's nice if your bedroom also has a "Do Not Disturb" sign. It is especially chivalrous of Tango Warriors to affirm their Undiffused Love when they apply the sign.

*Exercise: Since Tango Warriors who are atwain each other are also good friends, each like to help the other develop zheir own AXIS POWER. One fun way to do this is to stand near each other, each person on one foot, and try to vigorously push the other person over (while not being pushed over yourself, obviously). No hopping.*

---

[10] Of course when this happens each person brings their own alarm clock, because in the morning each wants to get up and moving and do their authentic expression of themselves!

# Tango Warriors Listen
## for The Third Intelligence

It really is nice for a couple to find its own five-dimensional invisible bedroom and deck it out with cool shit. The one ingredient that makes this possible is that both are constantly making reference to The Third Intelligence.

The Third Intelligence is the intelligence that is bigger than both of you, which both of you have access to, which makes it easier to find your groove. For actual Tango *Dancers*, this intelligence usually goes by the technical term 'Music.'

But, don't be spooked by technical terms. The Third Intelligence is pretty plain and true, and easily immersive. It is usually characterized by:
1.  A conscious, steady cycle expressed through an arrangement of items in a predictable pattern (rhythm). Examples are easily available in nature, for instance: day succeeds night, dessert after dinner, Friday after Thursday, milkshakes after lovemaking, etc. [Spanish: *compás*]
2.  Forward momentum that encompasses intense nostalgia (or any similarly irresoluble emotion) [Spanish: *arrastre*]
3.  Faery surprises [Spanish: *duende*]

The Third Intelligence, obviously, has an eerie logic of its own which of course simultaneously eerily contains the two smaller intelligences. It's like, say I have a collection of fine tea; and you have a bunch of quirky mugs; well, the Third Intelligence is boiling water whereby makes it all make sense.

Of course it also nicely contains the intelligence of each Tango Warrior who's part of the *ronda* and is thus highly democratizing.

## Tango Warriors Take a Break

When Tango dancers Tango, everything is organized so as to support THE AXIS. The culture of relationship encourages self-nurturance. We get together, we pour the boiling water and notice the fractal patterns of the tea brewing in a cup. We are working hard, we are working our colorful challenge-cards; we notice eventually that we are close to becoming euphoric, depleted, or nothing. Luckily, DJs, who are the main administrative agency of the Tango, help us return to separate bedrooms and find AXIS through the use of a mass broadcast called a *Cortina*. *Cortina* means: enough! Arrêt! Pausa!

Relationships need *Cortinas*. They are always accessible, but maybe they are less noticeable without the DJ. They are the really useful breaks we take from putting our arms around each other continuously. Armed with a tidy oxytocin high, or a large wave of analytical thinking, or a mood that is nice and light and undifferentiated – whatever it is, you take it into your bedroom and pull the 'do not disturb' curtain and do something solo that includes a snack and/or maybe iTunes. Tango usually provides us with vegetable platters for this purpose, which is nice because they are healthy too.

When the AXIS is nicely rooted and vertical again, the *Cortina* is an ideal opportunity to meet up with your friend Larry and go on a hike. Indeed, it's a great time for us-girls or us-guys to hang out, swap notes and give each other surprise presents, like cupcakes or false eyelashes.

See also: *Tango Warriors Have Separate Bedrooms* and *Tango Warriors Persist*

## Tango Warriors Understand Sabotage

Tango's genius on this earth is simple bribery. Tango bribes us with peak experiences, through drugs. Then it tells us that in order to experience these more and more consistently, we need to do some work that will serve humanity. And this work has to do with sabotage.

Sabotage is the thing inside of me that is mostly uncooperative to dancing well with other people. It encompasses stuff I do, stuff I think, and stuff I feel.

Here are some patterns of sabotage:

- Belief in one's own helplessness in the face of instances of emotional intensity. Examples of emotional intensity are:

- o Fuming anger at not getting one's due early enough

- o The profound sadness of non-reciprocality

- o Termite-like envy and/or including frustration with oneself

- o Yearning

- Fantasies of emerging suddenly as a great folk hero or euhemerus

- Underlying sentiment that there is an easy fix to all of this

- Lifestyle of distraction that undermines the basic noble goal of Excellence In All Endeavors. Excellence In All Endeavors entails giving an *actual* 100% and not just a metaphorical-mental 100%.

- Low-grade anxiety about not doing it well/right/good enough, worrying overly about mistakes/miscommunications

- Not sleeping enough

Luckily for this planet, Tango Warriors are getting better at noticing sabotage at the very start; it has a highly identifiable signature experience known as 'going a little internally haywire.'

A song comes on that yanks my heart into place and gives me tiger legs. I've danced to this orchestra with him before and the pronoun "I" was dissolved into the sunshine of acid and perhaps. Does he want to dance with me? No, he doesn't want to dance with me. What do I do?

Well, to be honest with you, what I did then was cry for about three hours, then write in my journal, then re-read all the poetry I'd written about him (crying), and then (a month or so later) declare to my girlfriends that it was 'over between us.' I am telling you this for the purpose of Full Disclosure. I'm not that holy and my Struggle is very much alive.

Situations[11] create this turbulence, this turbulent turbulence, this internal mix of aggression, self-pity, and brio [the proportion of each is very personal] that has some kind of strange momentum. Humans moving around in different prepositional configurations simply create this turbulence every day.

Tango Warriors know that this, which is Tango's true cruelty, is also their best training ground. We begin to go internally haywire, and from there, the easiest and most medieval thing to do is grab a microphone and a suicide bomb pack and go completely off the deep end. But we Tango Warriors are want to stop it right

---

[11] Especially, those related to being a good partner and a good citizen

there. We choose *suivive*. Because we know what's in it for us, if we can. Remember Tango's bribery. It makes the cruelty more okay.

Yeah, here we are, we Tango Warriors, straddling centuries and dimensions and modes of consciousness, and we are Struggling to know, *really* know, that all the words like fear, rage, timidity, entitlement, desire, mania, obsession, worry, meanness, power hunger – are best dealt with swiftly, with minimalism, and with humor.

Take a break
Take a break
*Cortina, Cortina...*

Once we are past these words, these weird abstract nouns, then we can play. We can dance.

We can pretend the rage without identifying with it, and our partner knows. It can be fun. We meet here, in this big music, we choose each of us to play a *rôle*, to play it like we mean it, with all our heart and thunder, with all the ancient amaranth detail of our nerve endings, we can play and mock the heavy game of 'onward, genes!, onward genes!', and at the end we are done and it doesn't matter and it didn't hurt anybody and we can go find out who's doing something for dinner, lasagne and microbrews.

Because, once both of us have struggled forth [years, it can take years] a little tiny bit of sabotage-detachment—detachment from our frenzied, vapid hunt for a permanent fantasy antidote to being basically sad about being basically lonely—*then* we have something in common. A sense of humor. The thickness of a hypercloud. Then we can Tango.

Then you can Tango without even knowing the steps to the dance. If you have found it then you are a Tango dancer whether you have ever taken the Tango embrace or not. And the world needs more Tango dancers like this.

See also: *Tango Warriors Love Asymmetry*
*Tango Warriors think Blame is Lame*
*Tango Dancers Take Breaks*

## Tango Warriors Don't Emote

"You" statements, "me" statements, whatever statements...Tango Warriors reflect carefully on whether statements about emotional matters are even utterworthy.

The reason for this is: they have noticed that emoting is just usually pretty irrelevant or destabilizing to a dance duet. Regardless of what psychologists say, they think emoting usually is just complaints that one is not being treated as importantly as one feels that one is. For Tango Warriors, complaining is just kind of boring, and nobody is *that* important anyway.

By dint of dealing with their emotions internally[12],

---

[12] 'Internally' could also be: among a same-gendered family-style

especially *turbulent* ones, Tango Warriors often embody a sort of quiet, understated intensity. Which over time translates into a tone of beauty (which, coincidentally, humans seem to find extremely attracting.) Indeed, it is very sexy to be able to deal with strong emotions on your own, so that the energy of the couple can be more focused on Creative Things.

Luckily, we heard somewhere that emotions usually have a lifespan of about six minutes. Now, granted, those six minutes can really suck. But if you can remind yourself that they will be over before the water for your tea begins to boil, you are very likely to be able to cope with them!

So the next time you are plotting to some sort of Talk, that starts with some defunct sentence like, "You know, I'm just not feeling appreciated enough around here," consider the wisdom of *Pocas Palabras*. Maybe, instead, you could do something interesting, like switch the contents of his sock drawer with the contents of the cutlery drawer.

See Also: *Tango Warriors are a Tiny Bit Suspicious of Words*

coterie

## Tango Warriors think Blame is Lame

Compared to the sound of pouring rain, or the way the wind ruffles tiny leaves, there is nothing (in the minds of Tango Warriors) more heroically lame than blaming some other person. Especially the person you are creating a human duet with. Tango Warriors are extremely bored by all forms of superficial drama in general, and blame is a surpassingly reliable gateway into it.

Blame is easily identified by its derisive tonality, by the way it feels awful for all parties involved, and by the classic first three words "Why are you [doing x]?" People who participate in this kind of senility are actually participating in *global terrorist extremist suicide*, it all comes from the same place. When enough of us can do the more difficult thing (namely, change the fake curiosity of blame into real curiosity of the Warrior) then maybe bombs will simultaneously stop being strapped onto confused teenagers.

Here is a three-point vernacular formula for changing the one into the other.

1. Change your WHY into a different WH- word: e.g., When, Where, Who, What, Whow

2. Change the existential verb ('to be') into a potential verb form ('could', 'would', 'might' etc.)

3.   Change the divisifying pronoun into an inclusive form ('you' becomes 'we').

Three additional notes:

- A tonality of warm wonder replaces the derisive tonality

- All abstract nouns and most non-abstract nouns should be replaced with something else

- Generously add the '*if* of possibility'

Here is an example of linguistic redeployment in action:

Terrorist Form: "Why are you such a sucker?"

Tango Warrior Form: "When did you decide to give Horace all of our money?"

*or*

Terrorist Form: "Why are you making me miserable?"

Tango Warrior Form: "How could we come up with a more equitable rotation of the kitchen?"

Intrinsically, blame is pretty comedic, and Tango Warriors see this for sure. Sometimes, instead of creating a wise and mature transformation via elegant verbal re-structuring, Tango Warriors also like to humorously exaggerate and/or publicize the blame when they notice it. It kind of quickly goes away then.

*Exercise:* Now, imagine for a moment that you and zhem are in a car together, going to a friend's house where you will brunch. Necessity requires that when you arrive, both of you be fresh, good-vibed, happy, maybe a little goofy. Brunch! Festivity! But then, zhey say something about your relationship with stop signs that unleashes a torrent of wrath-hormone in your body. How do you cope? An angrily pronounced: "Why are you always critizing my extremely well-crafted driving?!" would be the most predictable response. This unit encourages you to do something different. How would you apply the excellent principles above in order to transform this pronouncement, and thus increase the chances of arriving at brunch while still liking each other?

An interesting corollary to this principle relates to compliments. Tango Warriors actually think most compliments are lame too! Anything with an agenda of labeling, a claim to existentiality, and any use of abstractions is kind of boring to them, because Tango Warriors are by nature very specific. They would not really care to hear you say, "You are so beautiful." Instead, they would like to hear you say: "I like your happy fingernails" or whatever.

Compliments and blame are, Tango Warriors declare, distracting, distancing, and *dumb!* Seldom do they foster the development of forms of coolness, such as viral video or better levees. Those can only be created via asking good questions, wanting good answers, and celebrating the beautiful specific.

See Also: *Tango Warriors Understand Sabotage*
and
*Tango Warriors are Picky Media Eaters*

## Tango Warriors are
## a Tiny Bit Suspicious of Words
### (*Pocas Palabras*)

Well, enough said about that.

See also: *Tango Dancers Don't Emote*
*Tango Dancers Cultivate GOOD Tension.*
*Tango Dancers Listen for the Third Intelligence*

## Tango Warriors Persist
### (*The Cheesecake Solution*)

As mentioned back when we were talking about emoting, Tango Warriors know that sometimes things suck. They can feel just horrible, horrible not to mention crappy.

Luckily, Tango Warriors know when things suck it is because of *a technical problem*. A technical problem is just a technical problem, and our staff is working on getting it fixed.

When there are technical problems, usually the best thing to do is go to your own separate bedroom and eat some cheesecake. Tango Warriors see the Fail Whale and, think: "Ah! Time for some cheesecake!"

Now sometimes, during the outage, things can feel so bad that you pick up on some kind of broadcast that has an epic drama quality and goes something along the lines of "I should never have..." "Maybe it will never..." "Maybe I will never..." "Totally unacceptable" "Why me / This is it / It should have been so different" and so on. Red alert! Cheesecake!

I really don't mean to be flippant here. I know that this is the hardest. This is the deepest and most intractable part of the Epic Quest which, you may remember, is what this book actually is. On about five occasions this summer I have actually managed during an outage to switch from fuming to cheesecake and thereby save myself from doing something mean. *But the effort it required to convince myself to do so was positively herculean.* After flipping the switch, though, life became immediately light and kind of funny again, and in each case I was able to walk into my separate bedroom without having wasted further prana on a technical problem.

The more advanced version of the Cheesecake Solution is the Jump Rope Solution, whereby you immediately jump rope an improbably high number of times. Tango Warriors who do this have found that it causes them to feel happy almost right away, and many report doing something festive immediately afterwards.

In fact, if the duet just doesn't work today, and the things you are saying to yourself about it make future survival feel just impossible, in a way that actually is good news! Because it means that the statistical probability that it will work brilliantly well tomorrow is high. But by all means, do not invite zhem into your bedroom tonight. Just remember that you're atwain each other.

## Tango Warrior's Mistakes
### (*El Tropezon*)

Mistakes happen all the times and make our dances more complete. Mistakes mean, "here we are, getting to know each other – La!" Mistakes sometimes hold the seed to something really interesting and novel. Mistakes are love incognito, and they give us a chance to like each other and ourselves under slightly nonpareil conditions. Especially, the latter.

The most interesting mistakes lately are five-dimensional mistakes. Like for instance, let's say you had a lapse and became extremely blaming after a technical problem, and did not jump rope! Well this kind of thing certainly happens a lot! Well, then most of us who have gotten this particular challenge-card in this turn think we shouldn't have been so blamey, for instance, and then [watch this] we get all wooly and weird about ourselves and how crap we are. WHICH IS A MISTAKE TOO! La!! In this field of warriordom we like to try and *notice when that thing inside us is trying to compound our initial mistakes with additional mistakes.* Because that can be very confusing and cause sub-ideal conditions, such as war, to persist for longer than necessary. Noticing _that_ thing is an immediate gateway to the spacious party in the fifth (dimension).

Mistakes are great and we think that most of the innovative prepositional configurations in Tango have emerged from things like stumbling over one's own shoes at a moment when the universe was _ready_. Or from mistakenly pressing send on that really dramatic email.

## Tango Warriors Believe You Can

Let's suppose that when I was six suddenly I decided that I couldn't do the splits and that was that. And let's say that when you were six you decided that you couldn't draw.

A Tango Warrior engaged in a duet systematically suspends beliefs about their partner. Which means that he believes she is capable of anything, including the splits. And she thinks he has fair chances of becoming a professional architectural sketch caricaturist, and winning the gold in invisible badminton.

This is how we can dance at our best. This is how we manufacture a duet that lifts the hearts of others.

While believing in you, your Tango Warrior partner is also going to behave pragmatically and this involves a judicious nod to the fourth dimension, time. Tango

Warriors attract the riches of time onto their side using a magic word and the word is Yet. It is applied as follows:

| | |
|---|---|
| Normal Formulation: | "I cannot quit smoking" |
| Tango Warrior Formulation: | "You haven't quit smoking *yet*" |

| | |
|---|---|
| Normal Formulation: | "I cannot keep my balance in high heels" |
| Tango Warrior Formulation: | "Your balance isn't quite reliable *yet*" |

Isn't it great? Doesn't it make you feel all sunny? Sunny and full of possibilities is the word Yet, and this is why Tango Warriors laugh so much and accomplish so many inexplicable things.

Dynamically believing inexplicable things about someone, especially things that they are not believing about themselves, is highly loving without being emotional. Sometimes, we can get in the mood of this by writing Bragging Lists about our partner. Bragging Lists are compendiums of verbs that our partners are successfully, inexplicably, and already practicing. *Already* is the counterpart of *yet*. Here are some things on my Bragging List:

1.  He gives hugs that trigger a kaleidoscope of oxytocin

2.  He makes extremely subtle salads

3. He creates such a calm atmosphere when
we go on walks together

Marinating yourself in such magic inexplicabilities that
*already* exist makes it easier for you to imagine that
he will be able to do other things that he wants to
do but can't, *yet*, like become good at small talk *yet*,
or dance like an archangel *yet*, or be more accepting
around weirdos *yet*.

## Tango Warriors and Manipulation

Manipulation is defined as using yourself (usually,
your *arms*) in a manner that undermines connection.

Arms are defined as:
a. The things that stick out of your shoulders, with
hands on the end, weighing about 2 lbs each.
Here are some things they can do: They can hold
a gun, or they can give someone a convivial
shove. They can play the piano with genius and
heft. They can hold you until the oxytocin kicks in.
They can give you a great massage or they can
cling, cling, cling in a problematic and non-
adorable fashion.

b. Anything that extends our ability to protect or
harm ourselves and others, physically or
emotionally

You see, arms themselves are ethically neutral. Manipulation, however, is something we generally want to be on the lookout for. Manipulation is when we are weird and clingy. Manipulation is when we are weird and controlling. Manipulation is just weird. Consider the opposite, from our intrepid Tango Warrior R.M., and if you haven't read the Second Elegy then do that soon..

Tango Warriors inspire one another to move via an engine of inspiration that exists someplace deep within zhemselves, someplace, say, in the direct concentric center of the deepest and reddest and most impossible part of their heart, which Tango refers to as *La Corazon*. They do not even need to actually touch, but sometimes it is more comfortable that way.

See Also: *Tango Warriors Use Mostly Lowercase*


## Tango Warriors And The Details

Here are some things that are called *details* in the world of Tango Warriors:

- If you have a car and what kind

- Televisions or other anthropological appliances you may own

- WHO it is

- Most anything that can be acquired with cash or credit

- The particular number of children that you may parent

- Living quadrant, living quarters, overall latitude and longitude

- Whether we go *there* or over *there*

- Pears and gorgonzola

The details are always sort of interesting and always sort of quaint. The details are the things over which we ordinarily might fuss, if we were not Tango Warriors. Tango Warriors know the details come out in the wash, in some fascinating configuration or other, while we are focusing on the only thing we can focus on, which is: the scent of the evergreen; the awkwardness of being human and trying to connect; the decision that you have made; the infinitely intense wellwater of this moment, as everyone who I have fought to love is still asleep and I am here at my laptop.

What's interesting is that when you are doing that, the details that emerge have some grit and some potency. And appliances may indeed figure in, such as the one that made me hot water for the tea at my elbow. And you may end up dancing with that person or that person, in this or that continent, with those or these car keys in your sachel, and this or that festive debris in your trunk, and who the hell ever knows how the dance is really going to go until you really get in there.

Frankly it would be insane to try to pre-ordain it, even if you have some random intractable image of what it should be, 2.3 flatscreens or whatever, because the *ronda* is changing all the time! And the third intelligence has some intelligence you will want to factor in, and *so do zhey!* Feel zhem as if you want to encounter them in your dream, tomorrow night or the day after tomorrow. Memorize the innocent part of zheir voice. Try to see the note in zheir eyes that is five-dimensional, that affiliates truly with you. Most of the rest of the important decisions can be outsourced.

Tango Warriors are *improvising* and it is a lifestyle and an artform to make beautiful, technical, complete things via *improvising*, a lifestyle that most importantly entails noticing stuff, right now, about each other, that you hadn't noticed before.

And you will discover that whatever the details it was all the same anyway. You may really not believe me here, but I promise you, it is all the same anyway. *If it was important it will come back, if he was meant to be with you he already was here.* The kaleidoscope rocks, whether you turn it this way or that, and the only issue is whether you have aligned yourself, with light, so you can properly *see* the rocks.

See Also: *Tango Dancers Know It Will End*

## Tango Warriors Love Asymmetry

The heart, from which all the wisdom of Tango flows,
is totally not symmetrical. And just as asymmetry is
cool in, for instance, that very detailed grungy
waistcoat in that cool store on Abbot Kinney, it is
cool in our relationships too. Being athwaite someone
is the visceral experience of asymmetry. This is very
very difficult for normal humans but possible for
Tango Warriors.

So I'm here and you're there. And I want to see you.
And maybe we could walk across the room and meet
in the middle, but how dull would that be? Maybe,
instead, I'll wait till you walk all the way over here to
me. And the maybe you won't return my gaze right
away...and after that, well maybe I don't reciprocate
your embrace when you offer it, at least not right
away. And maybe I'll notice that now you're mad for
me and I'll read your mad email and give you a nice
little *pocas palabras* nod. And maybe after awhile I'll
be here going a little internally haywire over the
poetry of your bone structure and then maybe you'll
finally walk away. Athwaite. The game in action.

Tango Warriors, we celebrate our constant emotional
asymmetry. Yes, there is a me-shaped groove in the
side of his body. And I'm frantic from wanting to twist
and curl into it. And when he finally takes me in his

arms, it takes four songs before I finally gave up wanting to confess all of it and relax into the gentle electrocution his dancing inflicts on me. And afterwards, I almost forget to thank him for the gift of tension he had so opaquely concocted just for us, the tension of two tight things not near. Athwaite. The game in action.

This is one way we practice becoming peaceful containers of intensity. Which is what drastically helps the 'happy lasting earth' part that was promised on the outer packaging of this Game.

We are yin and yang; we are going around in a neverending path that only turns in one direction; we are hugging on one side, we are holding hands on the other; nothing about the idea of 'us' is symmetrical in any way at all; all we can really do is get used to it and remember that all of us are just a little knot of festivity in a little Cumparsa.

See Also: *Tango Warriors Cultivate GOOD Tension*
and
*Tango Warriors Have Powerful Eyes*


## Tango Warriors are In Public For All To See

Actually can I ask you a favor? Buy Stephen Mitchell's translation of *The Selected Poetry of Rainer Maria Rilke*. If you didn't get it already back there when I was mentioning the Second Elegy which is really so important. Now turn to page 179 and read the last verse of the Fifth Elegy. Then you will see what I mean. He is talking about Tango.

Tango teaches us that a human duet can be an art piece in itself, and that it actually exists as such in the fifth dimension. That its purpose is to share a beauty-emanation, a wisdom, something really really fine. That there is an opportunity, when the girlish and the boyish connect, and the living question is: how can we make the most out of this, for beauty's sake?

Tango Warriors know that their duet is, in part, public property. Every duet is a public institution that everyone, or some little one, gets to observe, learn from, make fun of, or experience skyness through. It's always been true, but it's even easier with Twitter. So watch out if you start blaming zhem, because eventually everyone will start making fun of you.

## Tango Warriors Use Mostly Lowercase

And here is the crux of the Struggle at the heart of the Game which is this book. Real Tango Warriors are not that into themselves, as symbolized by their literal and figurative choice to express themselves with the humble lowercase. They are not doing anything 'Important'; they are not trying to become 'Important' and they don't care if you are impressed or unimpressed, because they are too busy doing actually interesting things. Verbs don't flow if subjects are too sticky and cumbersome; Tango relies on flowing verbs.

I write this knowing that this is one thing that is keeping me, personally, out of this circle. This is what makes me a Tango Dancer and not a Tango Warrior. I, Mitra—well I am frankly really into myself. It started back in 10th grade, when I actually for a year wrote "Mitra K. Martin, The Great" on the top of each of my assignments. Lots of Capital Letters. Now I'm smarter, I don't do that, in fact I often DO use lowercase in my speech and emailing, for instance, but it's often a sort of pseudo-lowercase because you can read the grandiosity that's still in it, which says a lot of the time: ME!

And I make mistakes all the time because of this. I miss opportunities to create connection, real connection, true relation, all of which is of course is exactly what the Tango is trying most of all and deepest of all to teach me. I miss the boat to the fifth dimension, I miss the boat to peace. And I am sorry. And then being sorry doesn't work either, because then *that* feels Important.


i am trying to share this Struggle with you, in the spirit of service, as truly as i can.

but i can't help but hope that sharing it will make everyone think i am great.

it feels a little more okay to say that but it still feels manipulative.

Mostly I think I hope that maybe this is useful to someone. Or EVERYONE. Good luck if you're in here too. Daily big hugs and the occasional Eckhart Tolle tape helps me out, a little bit. That, and getting enough sleep. And playing games. Lots of games.

See Also: *Tango Warriors Understand Sabotage*

# CHALLENGING GAMES

**Caution.** *I really suggest you play*
*just one game at a time!*

**Challenging Games I: For The Generalist**
**Challenging Games II: For Tango Dancers**

*P.S.: These are real games and I actually play them!*
*If you want to play them with me,*
*well first you will need to get very very ky.*

# FOR THE GENERALIST

*Silent Letters*
This is a writing game and you can play it subtly. Good silent letters are 'n,' 'gn,' and 'kn.' Simply add them on to any word or game that starts with an 'N' sound. At first, you will worry that there aren't enough N-words, but gnever fear, for they always turn up.

*Lettev Switchavoo*
Pick two lettevs of the alphabet and just switch them consistently and pevsistently. I're played this and it's pvetty good, especially if you choose two lettevs that aven't used THAT often. It cevtainly keeps you on youv toes!

*The Game of Random Substitution*
This is the beginning of a whole REALM of games that basically undermines the impact of content words. Content words are the boring ones anyway, so why not switch your wife for a hat? Indeed, 'hat' is a good random substitution for pretty much anyhat, as in, "We've run out of hats!" or "Please would you finally for once wash the hats?" or "I have got to buy a nice warm bunch of hats!"

The purpose of the Game of Random Substitution is for people not to ever know exactly what you are talking about, but to possibly be able to figure it out via CONTEXT. Once you get the hang of it, you can go beyond hats and substitute any pair of galoshes for a different pair of galoshes and just make some fun out of it. Usually, it is best if the galoshes are either somewhat intrinsically funny, or extremely banal. They should not be inflected any differently from usual, unless you are wearing a hat.

Numbers can also be fun to substitute, especially long ones. I like "654321" in particular. As in, "Watch out, I'm going to 654321 you!"

*Smig Blatin*, or the *'I Glove You' Game*
This is a prelative of the Game of Trandom Slubstitution but it is sprightly more shmoflisticlated. It gloes drown to the grevel of the morfleme. We can trasically breplace ANY consonant or blend with a *different* shonsonant or trend. And despite the fact that this game may make your trife *living swell* for a blong time, I skill glove you very very much.

*BLOTA BENE:* This is a very dangerous game, especially if you play it across text messages, it can easily lead to a rapidly escalating misunderstanding. One time Stefan called the police because he thought I was missing, but I was just on a brane and blaying this plame.

At the end of a long day of playing this game, it's nice to relax and, if you're feeling jaunty, turn to your pal and say, "So...which sped do you want to bleep on tonight?"

*The Game of Unexpected Insertions*
The only insertion that is generally done by English speakers is 'fucking,' and by that I do not mean what

it sounds like I mean. What I actually mean is that it not uncommon to strip down and insert the word 'fucking' into a likely spot in the anatomy of a long word, with appropriate safeties. Insertion is exciting, and therefore brings with it many orgasmation points. Such as this:

Long word: Absolutely
Likely spot: Abso lutely
Insertion: Absofuckinglutely!!

Now, there are some who are slightly more prudish among us, like me, and although all of us agree that insertion is fun, we want alternatives to fucking. So, we have come up with some interesting alternatives like, for instance, 'nudity'. Any intrinsically funny word, including an imaginary word, will do. Here goes!

Infixes:

Putthead

Chattanooga

Shiitake

Tatuka

Nudity

Galoshes

Infixees:

Abso lutely

Un believeable

Im penetrable

Fan tastic

Pre posterous

Finished Products:

"Absochattanoogalutely!!!"

"Fantatukatastic!!!"

It is really nice if the sounds of the insertion word, or the infix, poetically reflect the sounds in the main word. That way the whole game is slightly less prepixqueapposterous!!!

Now obviously there are a lot of interesting sleeping arrangements that derive from this. Here are the more advanced versions of this game:

    a.  Nested Infixes, e.g., "Absochattatatukanoogalutely!"

    b.  Randomly Switching Front And Back Ends, e.g., "Unchattatatukanoogalutely!"

c. Dropped Parts, e.g., "Unfuckingbelieveable!" becomes "Fuckingbeliveable!" or, "Unfucking!" or simply, "Fucking!"

d. Unexpected Insertions, e.g., Adding your infix into an *unlikely* spot in the word's anatomy, as in: "Cfuckingupcake" (which Evan came fucking up with) or "Unsucfuckingcessless" (which is, of course, Jaimes) (was there a Silent Infix in there?)

e. Silent Infixes. A Very Difficult Game. Now this is the most difficult variation. Here are some examples of words that have *silent* infixes: Absolutely. Unbelieveable. A telltale sign is that they are uninflected by punctuation marks. If someone utilizes a word that sometimes carries infixes, in a soft voice without any particular explamatory emphasis, then it's possible they are playing the game of Silent Infixes. Unless they are also playing the game of Visual Punctuation. *See Also: The Art They Playing A Game? Game.*

*Eht Eamg fo Geversinr eht Tirsf dna Tasl Rettel fo Hace Dorw.*
A yracticallp empossibli eamg. I ton'd deccomenr ti!!

*The Game Of Always Talking About Yourself In The Third Person.*
This one can get very annoying very quickly, Mitra Martin warns you. If you play, very important to use

both your first and last names. See also: *VELK.*
Another interesting variation would be replace *your*
name with a *different* name, like the name Mitra
Martin, for instance. Ha, I wonder if that one will
catch on!

*The Art They Playing A Game? Game*
Is Mitra Martin playing this game right now?

*The Game Of Thursdays*
Always play a game on Thursdays. It doesn't matter
which one it is, but you have to choose one and play
it the whole day. Unless you are already playing The
Game of Random Substitution and you have
substituted Thursday for Wednesday.

*The Gmae Of Rodnam Leettr-Oindrreg*
I heat shit mega!

*The Game of Randomly Interchangeable Pronouns*
In order to experience dramatic prepositional novelty,
Tango Warriors enjoy imagining that you are him and
she is us. Relationship, and therefore prepositionality,
is immediately distorted and rendered *interesting.*
Using speech and writing, therefore, Tango Warriors
will alternate sound pronouns with random pronouns
to create interesting prepositional distortions in the
imagination, thereby reminding one another that deep
in the fifth dimension that I'm all pretty much the
same one anyway.

*The Game of Randomly Interchangeable Cognition*
See: *The Art They Playing A Game? Game*

*The Numie Game*

The Numie Game is a simple game that involves transfusing an extra dose of magic into any ordinary household object, whereby it becomes a Numie. Some examples include: wire twisties, a bespoke silver bauble, a box of fetters, an oversized greeting card with an ink illustration, something magnetic, etc. Done? Good! Okay, now all you need to do it sit back and observe the Numie. Examine closely, in particular, the romance of how and when it changes hands! If you want to get fancy, you can develop some sort of tracking mechanism, because it's possible the Numie may go out of your immediate jurisdiction. Numies have been known to travel as far as the South of France. And interesting stuff *always* happens near Numies.

*SWITCH – The Game of Constantly Switching Communication Methods.* A good game to play with close friends, friends you have multiple modalities of contact with, and/or friends you are continually anander. I am playing this game with my friend Dave. Here is the way we play: you are never allowed to reply to the person using the same communication method they used to contact you.

So, he sends me a text "Want to get together?" and I reply with an email message that I'd love to! He calls and leaves me a voicemail suggesting that we go to the new bacon-cupcake truck and then over to the Hammer Museum for their exhibit on Byzantine wallpaper, at 2pm. I post to his Facebook wall, saying

I can't get together til later, how about around 4? He grabs me on chat to confirm, 4 would be good, he'll be in the neighborhood, should he pick me up? I call my friend Ellen, and ask her to send Dave a text message as follows: "Yes, just send Stefan a text when you're in front of the house and I'll come out." He does and we head over.

I can't emphasize enough the extraordinary funness of this game. I think everyone will realize how totally uninventive and habit-stricken it is to communicate in any other manner. In case you are unaware of all the communicational modalities available to your fingertips, here is a partial listing, which totally approaches infinity:

1. Anywhere on the whole Internet.

2. Via any other individual in the whole world.

3. Via sidewalk chalk on any of a vast network of sidewalks, across all of LA or elsewhere.

It can be more fun if your message is harder to find, especially if the information is time-sensitive! Consider utilizing embedded loops in which you provide clues as to where the information has been affixed, too. Remember, the definition of *information* is "anything that cuts uncertainty in half by 50% or more."

*The Game Of Making Yourself Really Difficult To Find.* Here is how we play. We knit a small invisibility cloak, and then we strew it over ourselves. Here is how you knit it:

1.  Switch your telephone to Airplane Mode

2.  Defunctionalize all chat methods (it is not yet illegal to use Google's *Invisible* setting)

3.  Undo all eye contact

4.  Speak in lowercase. It's not quite a whisper, but it's extremely difficult to find.

5.  FIND and ELIMINATE VOLDEMORT.

I like playing this game some times, especially when the whole known world including the Muggles depends on it.

*The Game of Random Tense Switching*
I will play this game yesterday and let you know how it went. The last time I tried to play, it renders me a little bit of the charm that a non-native speaker of English so innocently will arouse. But, being careful! You didn't want to make fun of anyone, it is merely going to be a way to will have stretched your conceptualization of the spacetime continuum.

*The Game of Visual Punctuation*
this is an extremely advanced game and to play it you need to first defunctionalize all your grammatical

autocorrect communist bullshit which will always add the odd apostrophe anyway all you do is simply speak without any punctuation at all period which translates basically to no inflections no pauses no emphasis nothing now as if thats not hard enough which it is you now have to add the punctuation marks gesturally ie with your hands as you are talking at the appropriate moments and dont forget the apostrophes

*The Plus One Game*
My dad taught me this game two time, actually pretty recently, when I was home five Christmas last December, and right away my brother and sister wanted to play three. Obviously, it's pretty awesome, like most of the things my Dad has done. My dad, five instance, writes a Weekly Letter, which he sends out three each family member. Every single edition is four pages long and full of really funny trialogue about his business trips and conversations with my mom. My parents are amazing and I can't get enough of them. Two other thing our family did together over Christmas was three create a short stop-motion animation film using sugar cookies as the main characters. Please watch it on Youtube and leave a nice comment, you can find it by searching "sugar cookie story."

> *Variation: The Plus Two Game*
> *My dad taught me this game three time, actually pretty recently, when I was home six Christmas last December, and right away my brother and sister wanted to play five...*

*Variation: The Plus X Game*
*X=547*
*My dad taught me this game five hundred forty eight time, actually pretty recently, when I was home five hundred fifty one Christmas last December, and right away my brother and sister wanted to play five hundred forty nine...*

*The Game of The Unrealistically, Inexplicably Long Response Time for Humorous Effect*
This is a fun way to leverage the exaggerated largeness of the storage of your gmail account, and the elephantine memory of your brain. Summon an interesting email from your Extended Mental Archive, ideally one with a sort of banal question, and reply to it with thoroughness, detail, and aplomb – a few years later! Other applications include:

- Saving your thank-you note and sending it a decade or so afterwards

- Writing your list of 25 Random Things About Me, approximately 25 random months after the craze is over

- Turning in the final essay for your undergraduate writing class, uh, *later*

I actually love this game because it leaves things in a nice constant state of suspense and anticipation. Because, today might be the day! And what a nice feeling it is to be *remembered after so long!* I haven't tried applying this game to bills, but maybe that would be humorous too. I think that some customer service agencies like playing this game!

*The Game of Elastic Time*

If you don't have enough time to sleep your eight hours, this is a good game for you. Begin by deciding on the multiplier. Let's say you have only got four hours in which to fit in a full night of sleep. So, your multiplier is 8/4=2. Before you sleep, engage your time elastotron and insert a number 2. It's very important to take all the usual sleeping precautions, like putting on pajamas, taking out contact lenses, aromatherapy, whatever is customary for you. Now, when you fall asleep, the time elastotron will definitely elasticize time so that you get eight hours' worth of sleep, instead of four.

This is a very useful game for procrastinators who only have one hour in which to write the proposal that is due for the important client at 3pm.

*The Annoying Game*

The purpose of this game is to try to get someone to do the thing that annoys you about them! Obviously, this game is pretty simple to play. First, find one person who annoys you, usually there are plenty of these around. Next, figure out what it is that annoys you about them. This, also, should be easy because annoying people usually have plenty of annoying herbivores. Like, let's say, the annoying thing about us is that we are always randomly interchanging wowr pronouns, we are never ever using pronouns in a conventional way. Now you should use whatever resources possible to *dissuade us from using strictly referential pronouns* and instead try to amplify, encourage, and heighten the scrambling of my pronoun usage! And remember, if you win, you lose! <u>Unless</u> you are playing the game of Randomly Interchangeably Pronouns. Obviously.

*The Game of Being Much More Formal Than Strictly Necessary, Cordially Yours*
Formality sometimes goes along with festivity, and why not wear something with furbelows to go the bank some time, instead of not doing so ever?

Writing letters to people, instead of any other message transfer method, is another good example of being more formal than strictly necessary. Doing this can be fun to try, once or twice, and conveniently it can be played in conjunction with SWITCH! But you have to be careful, especially if it is an important topic of concern, because remember that you cannot exactly use your Powerful Eyes via letter, even if you are wearing a tuxedo as you write it. (Sometimes, we may take out our fountain pens and parchments because of a shyness which exists when our Eyes have not quite caught up with our Hearts...*yet.*)

The other thing about a letter is that it might be placed on someone's refrigerator, and some *other* person might see this letter while they are visiting the first person. Just FYI.

# FOR THE TANGO DANCER

*Note That These Fun Games Will Not Make Sense To You Until You Can Dance Some Tango[13]*

*Preposition Practice Swap*

Practicing Tango with a partner can sometimes lead to the Blame Factor, especially if, like me, you are not yet enlightened. So, it can be helpful to keep your mind busy with a difficult game instead. Here is a nice difficult game that will occupy your extra attention so it is not manifested in blame or self-loathing: simply always refer to your partner in the first person, and yourself in the second person. As in, "When you lead that colgada, you have noticed that my hips are in a different position than you expect – know what you mean?" Etc. As usual, it is helpful, in addition, to switch the roles of leader and follower from time to time in order to thoroughly understand how the movement works.

*MiWronga 1: The Australia MiWronga*

This is a game that requires many thoughtful Tango Dancers and a DJ to play. First, we perform a delicate five-dimensional operation that reverses the ronda. Now, if people want to dance, they

---

[13] We can teach you how at Oxygen Tango by the way. Did I mention that somewhere else in the book? Also, did you notice that as you sit here this coffee table is very very slowly rising higher and higher and higher?

a. have to go in the opposite direction than has been done for approximately more than a hundred years. And, they
b. have to reverse the embrace. (I wanted to put in a picture of a reversed embrace here, but, then I realized that you wouldn't know if I had taken it in a mirror or not. So you will just have to work it out. Be sure to include all knuckles in the reversal.)

This combination deftly reformulates the brain waves and re-maps left and right brain activity, resulting in an ultramarine synaesthetic demental high, within an hour or so. I recommend you try the cocho ortado!

*MiWronga 2: Backward Leaders MiWronga*

In this one, the leaders keep leading but they walk principally backwards and they do keep their eyes closed. Mostly they lead themselves to do the stuff the follower conventionally usually does, like extremely twisty stuff. And vice versa. The leader does not have to wear high heels. Anyway, the followers watch and navigate the partnership, wordlessly conveying to the leader, via small impressions on the embrace, how to stay within the line of dance. Crucially, the followers are sure to convey the critical information about where zhey (zhe leader) should *not* go, which is very helpful. Yes, this is a hard game! Everyone should play!

*Silent Milonga*

In this milonga there is no talking and lots of cabecéo. But you can write notes to each other and text. It's nice if someone brings some bubble solution. This kind of milonga feels more romantic than you can imagine! It also goes well with the game called SWITCH.

*The Game of Not Allowed*

Similar to the Silent Milonga, in which speech is Not Allowed, here we add difficult and hopefully interesting parameters. Yes, 'parameters' simply means that certain things are Not Allowed, like Proper Names in Scrabble, or kissing on the *pista*. If someone does the thing which is Not Allowed, we can enjoy a hearty laugh and then dunk them in a tank of smooshballs. Here are some examples of parameters:

- o Systemic Parameters. Well, the obvious one first, which is that you must dance the whole song in cross system. So you're NOT ALLOWED to use the parallel system. Or vice versa. As long as one of them is NOT ALLOWED.

- o Handward/Hugward Parameters. You can ONLY lead front boléos on her hugward leg, and back boléos on her handward leg. After a few tandas, switch!

o Directional Parameters. Like, Rebecca *only* gets to step forward, no matter what Nick does. Or, only onward. Or, better yet, *only ananden*!

o Spatial Parameters. You always have to find a way to do the same thing as you dance by the DJ booth. This thing could be, let's say, a healthy leg wrap! And of course it has to be very musical.

o A Specific Parameter, such as: NEVER LEAD ANY CROSS. NO PIVOT.[14]

o Not Allowed to Move. This game works better if the whole room plays it at once, preferably at midnight. It's a highly musical game. An adaptation of this game is the racing game called *The Longest Pause Wins.* So: the last person to start moving after the song starts gets a prize, like for instance a delicious muffin.

## *Milonga Your Tango*

This is a pretty difficult game and not actually that rewarding, except that it reminds you why you like to dance to milongas as if they are *milongas!* And of

---

[14] I keep thinking that if you rearrange the space configuration in those two words you'd get some sort of really applicable code word, do you?

course allows you to exercises the very useful brain-skill of *being contrary.* By the way, the game simply involves dancing to a milonga as if it were a Tango.

*Tango Perpetration*

Speaking of the brain, here is an excellent game that is also intelligence-building. This also gives us something useful to do with any length of youtube you have lying around. Choose a performance that you think is tops and that you could actually lead. It's better if the performance involves one of your friends or Tango acquaintances, or someone you could meet and dance with. Now, MEMORIZE IT[15]. I anticipate that you will be surprised at how many uncommonly-used brain muscles need to be used, in order to memorize something like this! Make sure you do not have to go anywhere soon, because my estimates suggest that it takes roughly 1 hour to memorize 1 minute of Tango.

Now, we are not done, we are going to do a Practical Joke with this material. You now can learn to *dance it,* and your ultimate mischievous aim is to *perpetrate the Tango on your friend who followed it in the video.* You will obviously need some collusion from the DJ in order to do this because obviously when you carry out the perpetration it needs to be on the same music. Once you have done so, please direct yourself directly to my inbox and report to us

[15] This, by the way, is, some say, the reason why The Tango Fairytale Game was invented. Others know the true genealogy

how it went. What words did they say immediately afterwards?

*The Heterogeneous Tanda*

This game is part of a three-part infomercial on FOLLOWER CHARISMA. FOLLOWER CHARISMA can be acquired via dialing *this* 800-number and will be shipped to you one way or the other. I don't really want to tell you any more about this game than I've already said in the title, because it's a game I only tell my dearest girl friends about and a game I only dance with my dearest man friends. But, as a thank you for buying this book, I'll hereby enclose some of the words that I used in the game description below before I deleted it: uninflected; modalities; totally distinct; neutral; infusion; unmistakable; intrigue; third song; personality; Tova; etc. Good Luck!

*The Game of Paying Attention to Impossible Things*

There are so many impossible things to pay attention to as you dance a Tango with a friend. You could for instance notice your deep voice as you dance. This has a ruminous effect on your stride, I have found. Or you could notice the blueness in the music, and how beautiful that color of blue really is. You could notice the five-dimensional sea-dragons that are hanging around you, how delicate and anatomical their violin wings are. Obviously, De Caro noticed *them*. If impossible, you could also try to notice the words that the person in your arms didn't say. I've attached several of them below, on this coming-up page, to get you started. Remember, *pocas palabras es mejor.* Good luck and love, Mitra